FORBIDDEN

MANIPULATION

THE ULTIMATE GUIDE TO LEARN HOW TO INFLUENCE ANYONE'S MIND USING NLP, PERSUASION, HYPNOSIS AND ADVANCED TECHNIQUES TO ANALYZE AND CONTROL PEOPLE

Table of Contents

Introduction

Manipulation is a form of social influence which uses indirect, underhanded, and deceptive tactics to change people's perceptions and their resultant behavior. Usually, the end goal is to advance the interests of the person who initiates the manipulation. In many cases, manipulation happens at the expense of the person that is being manipulated; they may be emotionally, mentally, or physically harmed, or they may end up taking actions that are against their own best interests.

It's important to note that social influence is not inherently bad; one person can use manipulation techniques for the good of the person he or she is manipulating. For example, your family members or friends can use social influence and manipulation to get you to do something for your own good. The people who mean you well might manipulate you as a way of helping you deal with certain challenges or to help you make the right decisions.

However, in this book, we won't focus on the garden-variety harmless forms of social influence. We are more interested in the kind of manipulation that is done with malicious intentions. This is the kind of manipulation that disregards a person's right to accept or reject influence. It is coercive in nature; when the person being targeted tries to push against it, this type of manipulation gets more sophisticated, and the end goal is to negate the person's will to assert for themselves.

How Manipulation Works

There are several psychological theories that explain how successful manipulation works. The first and perhaps the most universally accepted theory is one that was put forth by renowned psychologist and author, George Simon. He analyzed the concept of manipulation from the point of view of the manipulator, and he came up with a pattern of behavior that sums up every manipulation scenario. According to Simon, there are three main things that are involved in psychological manipulation.

First, the manipulator approaches the target by concealing his or her aggressive intentions. Here, the manipulator seeks to endear himself to his target without revealing the fact that his ultimate plan is to manipulate him or her. The manipulator accomplishes this by modifying his behavior and presenting himself as a good-natured and friendly individual, one who relates well with the target.

Secondly, the manipulator will take time to know the victim. The purpose of this is to get to understand the psychological vulnerabilities that the victim may have so as to figure out which manipulation tactic will be the most effective when he ultimately decides to deploy them.

Depending on the scenario, and the complexity of the manipulation technique, this stage may take anywhere from a few minutes to several years. For example, when a stranger targets you, he may only take a couple of minutes to "size you up" but when your partner or colleague seeks to manipulate you, he or she may spend months or even years trying to understand how your mind works.

The success of this second step depends on how well the first step is executed. If the manipulator successfully hides his intentions from you, he is in a better position to learn your weaknesses because you will instill some level of trust in him, and he will use that trust to get you to let down your guard and to reveal your vulnerabilities to him.

Thirdly, having collected enough information to act upon, the manipulator will deploy a manipulation technique of his choosing. This means that the manipulation technique chosen will depend on what the manipulator can stomach. A manipulator with a conscience may try to use methods that are less harmful to manipulate you. One that completely lacks a conscious may use extreme methods to take advantage of you. Either way, manipulative people are willing to let harm befall their victims, and to them, the resultant outcome (which is usually in their favor) justifies the harm they cause.

Simon's theory of manipulation teaches us the general approach that manipulators use to get what they want from their victims, but it also points out something extremely important: Manipulation works, not just because of the actions of the manipulator, but also because of the reactions of the victims.

In the first step, the manipulator misrepresents himself to the victim: If the victim is able to see through the veil that the manipulator is wearing, the manipulation won't be successful. In the second step, the manipulator collects information about victims to learn about his or her vulnerabilities. The victim may be able to stop the manipulation at this stage by treating the manipulator's prying nature with a bit of suspicion. In the third stage, the manipulator uses coercive or underhanded techniques to get what he wants from the victim. Even in this stage, the victim may have certain choices on how to react to the manipulator's machinations.

The point here is that when it comes to manipulation, it takes two to tango. By understanding both the victim's and the manipulator's psychology, it's possible to figure out how you can avoid falling victim to other people's manipulation, and it can also help you become more conscientious so that you don't unknowingly use manipulation techniques on other people around you.

Let's look at the vulnerabilities that manipulators like to exploit in their victims.

The first and most prevalent vulnerability is the need to please others. We all have this need to some extent; we seek to please the people in our lives as well as total strangers. This is technically a positive quality that helps us coexist in our societies, but to manipulators, it's a weapon that can be used against you.

Many of us are willing to endure certain levels of discomfort just to make other people feel happy; we feel a certain sense of obligation towards one another, and that's just human nature. The closer we are to certain people, the greater the need to please them. For example, the need to please your friend is higher than your need to please a stranger.

Manipulators understand this, and they use it against their victims all the time. If a manipulator wants to get something big out of you, he will first take the time to get closer to you, not just to get to know your vulnerability, but also to increase the sense of obligation that you feel towards him.

The second vulnerability is the need for approval and acceptance. Again, as social beings, we all have an innate desire to feel accepted. We want people to love us, to think of us as members of their groups, and to choose us over other people. This feeling can be addictive, and it can give other people (especially manipulative ones) a lot of power over us. The vast majority of manipulation victims are people who have close personal relationships with the manipulators; in other words, they have an emotional need to gain the acceptance or approval of the manipulator. The remaining manipulation victims can be manipulated because they want to be a part of something (a group, a social class, etc.).

The third vulnerability that manipulators like to exploit is what psychologists refer to as "emetophobia" (which is the fear of negative emotions). To some extent, we are all afraid of negative emotions; we will do lots of things to avoid feeling angry, afraid, stressed, frustrated, and worried, etc. We want to lead happy and fulfilled lives, and anything that makes us feel "bad" is a threat to that sense of fulfillment. So, in many cases, we will do what manipulators want if it serves to alleviate that "bad" feeling. Manipulators know this, and they use negative emotions against us all the time.

The fourth vulnerability is the lack of assertiveness. Assertiveness is a very rare quality; even people who you may generally consider to be assertive are likely to cave in if manipulators push hard enough. Even when you are willing to stand your ground and to say "No" manipulators can be very persistent, and in the end, they can wear you out.

The fifth vulnerability is the lack of a strong sense of identity. Having a strong sense of identity means having clear personal boundaries, and understanding one's own values. Unfortunately, these qualities aren't so strong in most of us, and that leaves us open to manipulation. Manipulators succeed by pushing our boundaries little by little, making them blurry, and then taking control of our identities.

Finally, having an external locus of control, and having a low level of self-reliance are also key vulnerabilities that manipulators love to exploit. When you have an external locus of control, it means that your identity and your sense of self are external to you. It means you view yourself through other people's eyes. It means that you are extrinsically motivated. When you have low self-reliance, it means you depend on other people for sustenance and for emotional stability. It means that if support systems in your life are taken away, you can easily find yourself leaning on a manipulator, which leaves you at his mercy.

Chapter 1.   Become A Manipulator

Is language the primary tool of deviously manipulative people? How can words have such a powerful effect on us?

How a manipulative person mind works, is most likely only something a manipulative person could comprehend. The rest of us look on in confusion, wondering why or how someone could behave this way. Though, in some small way, we can all be a little manipulative at times. For example, most people will be willing to bend the truth, or omit information, on the odd occasion. For much the same reasons, such as trying to get others to do something for them or even to get permission for something. Trying to convince someone of your argument or to get them to come around to your way of thinking, is a natural and evolutionary process. Pinker and Bloom (1990) argued that we evolved to use language because it helped us to adapt to our environments. Surviving hostile elements is easier if we can persuade others to help us persevere.

The use of language to manipulate others to help us is the evolutionary adaptation, it appears to be a natural process. Why then, do some individuals manipulate others for more perversive means? Not for survival or evolutionary means, but purely for their own selfish needs. If they cannot achieve this control, they feel helpless and lack any agency in their lives. Why is this? Are they evil, are they unkind, are they born that way? Some might say it is a personality disorder that is bordering on a narcissistic level.

We will all try to persuade someone at some point in our lives, but we are not all narcissists. Whatever the reason for our attempts at persuasion, we usually want to remain on good terms with the person we are trying to manipulate. Not so for those who manipulate to control.

Kier Harding, a lead Mental Health practitioner, wrote a relevant article in The Diagnosis of Exclusion. He argued that those diagnosed with a personality disorder are actually people who are not very good at manipulating. Their attempts tend to be forceful and over exaggerated.

Whereas a skillful manipulator will aim to persuade someone less overtly. It is because they are not very good at it, that makes them unlikable characters with poor interpersonal skills. Usually also with a low self-esteem because of their background in life. This could be an argument indicating that controlling manipulators are from dysfunctional backgrounds.

How then can we recognize such a deviant person?

Common Traits

Use of Language

We have shown how powerful language can be, as a prime tool of persuasion. There is more to the manipulative controller than mere words. They will use tactics that mislead and unbalance their target's inner thoughts. We now understand that through language, they will:

- Use mistruths to mislead and confuse their target's normal thinking pattern.
- Force their target to make a decision at speed, so they don't have time to analyze and think.

- Talk to their target in an overwhelming manner, making them feel small.
- Criticize their target's judgment so they begin to lose their own self-esteem.
- Raise the tone of their voice and not be afraid to use aggressive body language.
- Ignore their target's needs, they are only interested in getting what they want and at any cost.

Invasion of Personal Space

Most of us set boundaries around ourselves without realizing we are doing so. It is a kind of unspoken rule to protect our own private space, such as not sitting so close that you are touching another person, especially a stranger. A manipulative character cares nothing about overstepping such boundaries. Whether this is because they do not understand, or they do not care is unclear. Initially, they are unlikely to invade their target's personal space. They will seek to build up a good rapport first. This shows that they do understand boundaries because once they gain the confidence of their target, they will then ignore them.

Fodder for Thought

Manipulators tend to be very ego-centric, with limited social skills. Their only concern is for themselves. Everything they do in life will be in relation to how it affects them, not how their actions affect others. Does this mean that they have a psychopathic disorder?

Take empathy for instance. Controlling manipulators are unlikely to ever show empathy. Empathy is a natural human emotion that aids in our survival techniques. A study by Meffert et al. indicates that those with a psychopathic disorder are able to control empathetic emotions. They lack sympathy of any kind because another weakness is simply another tool for them. When they detect any weakness in their target's resolve or personality, they will exploit it. The consequences to their victim are of little importance. The targets weakness's feed the manipulator's strength, making them bolder and often crueler in their actions.

Creating Rivalry

Another tactic of the controlling manipulator is backstabbing. They may tell you how great a person you are to your face, making themselves look good. Behind your back, they are busy spreading malicious gossip and untruths about you. This is a classic trait of a controlling manipulator as it creates a rivalry between people. Then, they can pick sides that will make them look favorable, particularly to their target. It can act as the first stage to getting close to their target. Once bonded, they can start to build up trust, making it easier to manipulate the target in the future. If you recognize a backstabber, keep them at a distance. Their agenda is selfish so it is better not let them into your personal life. There is no point treating them as they treat you, in revenge. It will turn out to be exhausting playing them at their own game. If they know that you are on to them, they may attempt to lure you back with praise, remember that it is false.

Domineering Personality

It is unlikely that a manipulative person will outwardly show any form of weakness. An important part of their facade is to show conviction about their views. They seek to impress, believing they are right about everything. Almost to the point that if they realize they are wrong, they will still argue that they are right. On a one-to-one level, that invariably means that your position is always wrong. As they will chip away at your beliefs, they seek to undermine your sense of self-esteem. Once they have achieved this, then there is no holding them back. They seek to domineer others, often speaking with a condescending tone to belittle their victims. Using ridicule is yet another tool against their target, merely because it will make themselves look better. If you ridicule them back, they will seek to turn the tables, accusing you of being oversensitive to their "joke." The kind of joke that only the teller sees the funny side of.

Passive Aggressive Behavior

A common trait of many hard-core manipulators is passive aggressive behavior. Because they prefer to be popular, they do not wish to be seen as doing anything wrong. Not that a manipulator would ever admit to doing anything wrong. They are experts with facial expressions that are meant to dominate and to intimidate. This may include; knitting eyebrows, grinding teeth and rolling eyes. It may also include noises such as tutting and grunting sounds. It is a very common behavior for such a character, as there is little anyone else has to say that they will agree upon. For most manipulators, it is their life's ambition to show people up by proving them wrong.

This can range from the confrontational look, where they seek to stare their target down. Or, it could be in response to their disagreement on something their target said. They may smirk and shake their head, turn their back, anything to show their strong disapproval. It is all a ploy to make themselves look superior and put others down.

Moody Blues

What of emotional stability of the manipulator? Is it that which makes them behave the way they do? Do they even know what happiness is? The answer to that is a most definite yes, at least to the latter.

Happiness is a tool used initially to help them manipulate, a happy target is more likely to comply. This, in itself, makes the manipulator happy, or at least in a sense of what they consider happiness. But their joyfulness is a perverted model of what most others consider happiness to be. Their happiness is often built on the foundations of another's misery. A misery that they have caused with their cruel manipulations. Equally though, a manipulator is prone to mood swings. Most likely to happen when things are not going to plan. One minute they are euphoric at their latest conquest. Then next they could be completely deflated at their failure to succeed. One thing is certain for those who live with or become a target of this type of domineering character, they will be unhappy all the time.

Intimidation

One aspect of manipulation, often used as a last resort, is intimidation and bullying. When everything else has failed, they begin to use threats to get their own way. Some though may use intimidation from the onset. It may in a source of authority. For example, let's take the role of a manipulative boss. You have requested a day off. They don't want to allow you your request but have no choice, it is your right. This type of person would want their pound of flesh first. They will set goals for you to reach so it will delay or cancel your request, such as moving project deadlines forward. This way they have their little victory over you.

Alternatively, such a manipulator may use the tactic of the silent treatment. Ignoring someone to the point that it becomes obvious you have displeased them. They seek to make you feel the guilty party.

Other more direct intimidating actions may include stance. Using their height or build to tower over you, or standing uncomfortably close.

Be careful as they will seek revenge for wrongdoings they perceive done to them. Nothing will go unnoticed under their watchful eye. Everyone is a potential target. But, the weak are more likely to walk into their traps, because they are the ones who are easier to dominate. The vulnerable will have little resistance and are easier to bully and coerce. Many of these traits seem more fitting to men, but women can be cruelly manipulative too.

This is a person who will never back down in an argument. Never admit they are wrong. Never apologize for anything. A manipulator will never show respect but will expect everyone else to show them respect.

They love nothing more than to embarrass others. Playing the dumb one is common practice, just to force another person to explain themselves further. At every opportunity, the manipulator will jump in with some sarcastic remark, "hurry up, we're all waiting for your intellectual explanation" or "why has no one else ever heard of this?"

Their sole aim is to make the other person look a fool, but without seeming to be the one who made it happen. Oh no, the victim did that to themselves because they are stupid.

So, what of the victims of such a manipulator? Let's now move on to the other side of this role.

Chapter 2.   Manipulation Techniques

There are literally hundreds of techniques that manipulators implement in order to get their way. Some are manifestations of their own personality played out in real time, while others are tried and true methods of persuasion and manipulation. Some of them are actual techniques researched for their ability to produce high-quality results within corporate or business settings. It is a stark realization that techniques of manipulation are used on people across the spectrum.

Manipulation within a corporate environment isn't a technique written in the handbook or taught in any class. They usually start from the top down and then are mimicked within the ranks because they are found to be successful at producing the quality end result needed. Those looking to move up the corporate ladder might find themselves using these techniques simply out of wanting to move up. While others use them for their own self-gratification.

Whether you are looking to implement these techniques for your own purposes or are attempting to understand them in order to not fall victim, the following information will give a full understanding of the research behind them and the probable situations used. Those with little manipulation skill or moral withholding to employ them, might find themselves in a bad situation for everyone involved. While you may learn the ins and outs of some of the techniques, remember that they are often used in very unforeseen circumstances such as charity drives, promotions, financial obligations, and even in places such as religious institutions. No one is clear and safe from manipulative techniques but if you become aware of the most widely used, you may be able to escape without falling for the manipulation at hand.

The Fear-and-Relief Technique

The Fear-and-Relief Technique is explained in the title alone. This technique combines both negative and positive actions. The point of the technique is to introduce some sort of situation or dialogue to the victim that would put fear or anxiety into their system. The plot has to be solid enough to have that situation at hand affect them in the immediate moment. For example, You are the Manager of a department inside of a corporation. You know that the job you have is outside the scope of your employee's job description. You know the employee is not willing to work outside of the job description. So, you first introduce the fear. You may specifically target the employee, saying their work ethic has decreased and there are future layoffs coming. This will have them fearful for their job, which to them, translates to food, care for their families, their home, their children and so on.

The second part of the fear-and-relief technique is to then introduce something that may offer some relief but is not something in a normal situation you could ask for them to do. Using the example above: Your employee is distraught, frightened, and worried about their livelihood. The manipulator then turns the tables, giving the employee a comforting talk. They let them know they don't want to see them go, often lying about their emotions for that employee. The manipulator then comes up with a "brilliant" idea. There is a project that normally would not fall on them, but if they volunteer to take care of it, it would show they are more important to the department than any other employee. The manipulator might even promise to put in a good word for them during evaluations. This employee is so relieved that there is a way to save their job they not only take the extra responsibility but they thank the manipulator for helping them out.

The Mirror Technique

The mirroring technique is sometimes used without even knowing. However, for a master manipulator, it can be one of the easiest ways to gain trust from a person. There are two levels of this technique. To begin the manipulator must choose their target carefully, knowing they will be capable of lowering their own physical personality to reach the targets. This technique is quite often used by narcissists but has been employed in such things as interrogations, and interviews by journalists.

The manipulator then begins to mirror the other person. It is a subtle change, first focusing on their body movements. Crossing arms, legs, facial expressions, posture, etc. Then the manipulator moves on to their speech patterns and habits. If the person has a low calm tone, the manipulator moves theirs to match. If the target has a loud boisterous personality, the manipulator will slowly move theirs up to match. Often times, for master manipulators, they are even able to mimic things like accents and breathing patterns.

The point of the mirror technique is to attract trust from the target. Without knowing it, as you begin to mirror every aspect of the person in a subtle manner, the target starts feeling as if they are seeing themselves in the manipulator. There is nothing more comforting than your own persona. This allows the target to relax a bit and begin to trust the manipulator more than before. It can be a very powerful technique. Within the public, this technique is often implemented by Police, Military, and during such events as hostage negotiations.

The Mirroring technique is also taught to select groups of people, such as special forces military, spies, and black operatives for use in their work. These techniques not only bring comfort, but they bring empathy. When the target sees themselves in the manipulator, they are then more likely to empathize with the manipulator. This allows for manipulation to begin. When the target has removed all suspicions or nerves with the manipulator, sees themselves in them, has a sense of empathy, and trust them, the manipulator can see the core of that person and in turn, exploit them for their own personal purposes.

The Guilty Approach

The guilt approach can be combined with other approaches such as the mirroring technique for the best results. The guilt approach is when the manipulator uses one of several different techniques to bring about the feeling of guilt in the target's emotions. They may unreasonably blame them for something that has happened. They may target their emotion soft spots. Or they may even begin to put the blame of their own success or failures on the target themselves.

In order to accomplish most of these, the manipulator must know the target pretty well. They must have earned their trust. They must know how the target will react and change their tone or tactics accordingly to get the best reaction from them. The point is not to anger the target but to make them feel genuinely responsible for what the manipulator is putting on them. They must have empathy for the manipulator and trust them enough to believe they are telling the truth.

This approach is used for both physical or financial gain, and for a boost in the manipulator's self-esteem. The guilty approach brings up feelings of good will, obligation, protection, nurturing, or instinct toward the manipulator. They then can take those and exploit them to get the outcome they were looking for. They may extort those feelings and receive a financial gain from it. They may turn the target against someone else which will ultimately lead to the manipulator's gain. They may also use the person's empathy to stroke their own ego and make them feel as if they were worthy of the praise.

In more dangerous situations, this technique can be used to twist the target into doing something heinous or nefarious. Having them kill someone for them. Having them take the blame for something they didn't do. Putting their own lives on the line for the manipulator who walks away free and clear. Oftentimes a manipulator can use this tactic on parents of a child who has been killed or kidnapped. They can use it on boyfriends to get revenge on someone that has hurt them in the past. The Guilty approach is used all of the time, even in small situations where someone who is ill uses that illness to obtain free things and advantages they would not have had otherwise. It is manipulation through emotion, one of the most powerful directives we have.

The "Victim Card"

The victim card, in many opinions, is one of the more egregious methods of manipulation. But before we talk about the manipulative form of this, let's clear up the other end of the spectrum. There are people who have undergone serious traumatic events that, due to psychological affliction from the event, are stuck in a perpetual rotation of self-victimization. These people are not consciously attempting to manipulate anyone. They are truly suffering from PTSD or other mental illnesses due to the trauma they perceived. From that, they are unable to pull themselves from this place without psychological intervention. Some of the signs of someone with a true victim status are:

- They struggle to take responsibility for their own actions or thoughts.

- Their life has not moved on from the event, especially inside of their mind.
- The anger they held from the event still holds true long after the event is over.
- They believe that controlling their own lives is impossible.
- Oftentimes this will lead to manipulation because the victim feels powerless in their own lives.
- Trust is not an easy thing for them.
- They are always on the edge of their emotions and tend to argue quickly.
- They have a negative self-image and feel sorry for themselves.
- They feel as if everyone else around them has more or has what they want. They compare themselves to others.
- Their attitude is always negative, glass half empty, about every situation
- They believe their life is not being lived to the fullest.
- They often defend their right to be a victim to the death.

- There is often a solitude they put themselves into, cutting family and friends out of their lives.

If you know a person like this, it is best to help them find professional help and therapy. Oftentimes therapy will help them push away the victim status and take their lives back into their own hands. Now, when it is not a situation of true victimhood, it can be a serious case of manipulation.

When it comes to master manipulators the signs are a bit different than the above. Oftentimes the manipulator will talk about their issues but never directly ask for what they need or want. They will skirt the issue, dropping hints, giving stories of how hard things are, but never come forward and directly say what they need. It sometimes confuses the target in knowing what exactly they want. Other times, it chips away at the target's goodwill, resulting in their offer to help with whatever is needed.

When a target is with a manipulator playing the victim, they will find that they feel guilty almost every time they are with that person. When you have conversations with them you are left feeling guilty, but you aren't exactly sure what you feel guilty for. There is a ball in the pit of your stomach and a general uncomfortable feeling.

The manipulator will point out other people's actions, downfalls, or even manipulation. They will always justify their own with a basis in the situation in which they experience. If the target criticizes them in any manner, the manipulator will immediately attempt to make the target feel selfish or guilty.

But I Love You So Much...

The form of manipulation also goes along with, "If you really love me." Both are used primarily in close relationships where both people know each other very well. Oftentimes, due to the relationship itself, it is hard to figure out whether or not you are being manipulated or not. When the person uses either of those phrases to get what they want, it is manipulation. Healthy relationships center around talking and coming to a common ground, not manipulating to get what they want. This can happen between couples and between children and parents.

If you are confused about whether your relationship is a manipulative one or not, there are some pretty standard things you can look at. First, is your relationship clear and concise or is it often hard to manage and difficult to navigate? Good relationships should be clear and concise. You know the person, they know you, and you don't feel the need to bribe or manipulate to get what you want. You know simple conversations will yield the right result for both of you. Manipulative ones can be confusing, disjointed, and complicated to understand.

Secondly, if you are constantly being blamed or shamed for your choices. If you are being bullied by the other party, this is usually a manipulation technique for both control, and to push you where they think you should be in the relationship. Bullying is not okay, nor is the blame game. It's not about who is right or wrong, it is about how to fix the problem and move forward.

Third goes along with the second thought in that control is not part of a relationship. In a relationship, you are two individuals coming together. You are not "becoming one" as the wedding vows say, you are still two different people with ideas and dreams. Ideally, they will coexist with your partner, but when they don't, you will be able to tell if the other is attempting to control you or not.

One of the other ways to figure out if you are in a manipulative relationship is to look at all the small faults you each have. Is it never putting clothes in the hamper? Is it never putting dishes in the sink? There are small things that bother us all about the people we spend the most time with. A healthy relationship will involve discussing them, and also finding the humor in those little things. A manipulative relationship will often be filled with nitpicking. Every little thing you do is put out there in a negative manner by the manipulator making you feel uncomfortable and self-conscious. This is a control tactic.

Unfortunately, if you are having to hear the words, "I love you so much" or "Don't you have a heart?" or "But I thought you loved me" then there is a good chance that you are becoming the victim of manipulation. It is not always the end of the world. It could simply be they really want something and are afraid to ask for it, but either way, it should be immediately addressed.

Bribery

Bribery, one of the most widely used forms of manipulation on the planet. There isn't a single person who hasn't used bribery at some point in their lives. Whether it's, give me your allowance and I won't tell mom you hit me, or promising your child an entire cake if they just sit still in church for ten more minutes, you are using bribery. Of course, there are all types of levels of bribery. There is financial bribery, criminal bribery, political bribery, and the list goes on and on. Bribery includes the manipulator giving the target something (usually money) in order for the target to do something for them in return, something that will allow the manipulator to highly profit from the venture.

Chapter 3.   Why Is Manipulation Important in Life

As we have been talking about so far in this guidebook, there are a lot of different scenarios that you can use manipulation in, and there are a lot of effects that can happen as a process as well, depending on how the manipulation is used. While we often think of manipulation as a bad thing, but there are actually quite a few benefits that are going to come with using manipulation in order to get what we want.

Just because we are getting what we want doesn't mean that we are going to always harm someone else. And this is the difference between regular manipulation and what is known as dark manipulation. It is an important distinction that we need to make. With regular manipulation, we want to get something, but we don't want the other person to get harmed or hurt in any manner, whether it is physical, mental, or emotional.

On the other hand, when it comes to dark manipulation, it isn't going to matter to the manipulator whether the other person gets harmed or not. They don't really care how much that person is harmed, and usually, there is going to be some kind of harm in the process. As long as the manipulator gets the thing that they want, they are going to be happy about the situation.

With that said, whether you are using manipulation in order to progress your own agenda while helping others (like in sales or getting some help on a group project), or you are using it to benefit yourself and you don't care if someone gets harmed in the process, there are going to be some benefits that come with using manipulation on a regular basis. Some of the benefits you can look for will include:

Manipulation is often going to work. The idea here is that if I know what I want and I know how to evoke a feeling in the other person so that they are more likely to do what I want, then manipulation is going to be effective, and we are able to measure this effect as well. Think of how this works. Businesses are going to spend billions of dollars in research to do various marketing strategies to point to how well the manipulation that is found in their campaigns and their advertisements work, so we know that manipulation must be something that works.

Of course, you have to do things the right way. it is not enough to just put an ad online or on television and assume people are going to come in droves to purchase the product. There is just too much competition out there, and often we see so many advertisements that it is impossible to just see something and be manipulated by it. There has to be another level, and there needs to be some experience and expertise to pull it off, and that is what the research dollars of many companies are spending on.

The same idea can be said when we take a look at regular manipulation that an individual is going to use. It is not enough for us to walk up to someone and say, "Do what I want!" The target is likely going to take a look at us and just laugh and walk away. And you would do the same as well. You need to make sure that you are using the right techniques, and that you really understand what the other person will respond to. When you use manipulation in the right manner, and with the right techniques you will find that it actually works which is a really cool benefit.

The next benefit that comes with manipulation is the idea that we can become pretty good at it. In fact, it is likely that you saw at least a few times when you have used manipulation in the past to help you get what you wanted, even if the answers ended up surprising you in the process. This manipulation is actually something that we have been practicing since before we were able to walk.

This is because there was a time when we were not able to walk, and we still needed to get things. We needed food something to drink to feel loved to have clothes, to get baths to get diapers changed and more. Even though we were not able to talk and voice our opinions on our own, and we were not able to take care of these things on own at this time, we were able to use manipulation in order to influence mom and dad to do the work for us.

Since we have been able to read others since a young age in order to help us get what we wanted as a baby up through adulthood, we are already good at reading others, often much better than we would think. And we can even find that, with a bit of practice, we are able to quickly guess the right thing to do to help us motivate that other person in the process as well. Of course, some of us are going to be much better at doing this than others, but it is still something that we can work on to improve and see some great results with influencing others.

Easier to get what we want. If you decided to come right out and ask the other person to give you exactly what you wanted, it is likely that they are going to say no. If you just ask about it, without using any of the techniques that we will discuss in this guidebook and the techniques of manipulation, then the other person really has no need to help you and won't feel guilty about doing something that they have no interest in helping out with.

However, if you are able to use some of the manipulation tools and techniques that we have been discussing so far, and you are able to trigger some feelings in the other person, you will find that it is easier to get the other person to do what you want. They are going to feel some kind of obligation to help you, even if they are not sure what that is all about. And even if they are not fond of the idea of helping you out, they are more likely to say yes.

This is going to be really great news for you. It means that you are going to be able to get the other person to say yes to what you want them to do, without having to push too hard or worry as much about whether they are going to say yes or no to you. You will have already put in the work that is needed to convince them to work with you, and it is likely, especially if you spent time analyzing them and using the right technique for their needs, that they are going to agree to what you want.

And the final benefit that we are going to take a look at here when it comes to using manipulation and some of the different techniques that come with it is the idea of power. Since all relationships whether they are with family, at work, or an intimate relationship, are going to have some element of power involved with them. All of us would like to have power over others or at least over someone at some point, and manipulation is going to be the tool that we need to ensure that we gain that power over our target.

Now, there are those who will take that power and go too far. This is where the manipulation is going to turn into abuse and some other problems as well. But the power that comes with manipulation can sometimes be as simple as having a bit of control over one person in your life, even your child, and it doesn't always have to be an abusive or negative kind of thing to work with.

The negatives of manipulation

Of course, there have to be a few negatives that come with manipulation. If there weren't, then everyone would use this technique all of the time and we wouldn't have some of the negative connotations that come with it along the way either. The negatives of this are going to mainly occur when you are not versed well enough in using manipulation or if someone catches you in the act of manipulating them. We will explore these a bit more as we get through these sections. Some of the different negatives that can come with using manipulation in your own life can include:

Manipulation is something that has the potential to backfire quite a bit. People are often going to have some kind of sense about when another person is trying to manipulate them. This is because we are heightened to the idea that because we want something out of another person, it is likely that someone else is going to want something out of us as well. When someone starts to sense that they are being manipulated, it is not going to end well for you and it is often going to generate a lot of anger, resentment and more.

If the target senses that the manipulator is trying to take control, or they feel that the manipulator is trying to take some power over them in a sneaky manner, it is likely that the target is not going to trust that person any longer. At this point, if the target feels like you have successfully manipulated him, he may withhold something from his manipulator in order to get even, even if it is not that big of a deal what you are trying to get. And if the target thinks that this manipulation has gone even further and feels like his feelings are being toyed with, then it is sure to bring out a big power struggle between the two people in this game, and the trust is going to head right out the window.

Another negative to be careful about is that we often are not going to think through the manipulation that we are doing before we do it. Before we even have a good idea of what we want out of the relationship, or before we start to evaluate the possibility of just coming out to the target and asking for what we want in a direct manner, we are going to head right over and start manipulating the other person.

The reason that we do this is because we are so eager to try out the techniques, we are eager to get what we want, or we just assume that the other person will say no to us and we don't want to worry about the rejection in the process. This step though is going to lead to some assumptions that you both that could end up corroding the relationship that you are in. Remember that once the relationship is gone and corroded, it is impossible for you to regain the control that you need in order to manipulate that person again.

There are a lot of different indirect versions of manipulation that can come into play, and sometimes they will become almost a habit in the relationship. Some of these are going to include options like guilt tripping, abusive criticism, and complaining. And another layer of the power struggle is going to start showing up in the relationship when we use these techniques all of the time, even though that was usually not the intention.

The best way to avoid this kind of issue is to make sure that you don't jump into the manipulation too quickly. You need to be able to think it all through properly, and really consider when you will use it, how much you will use, how you will manipulate and more. Manipulation is something that has to be thought out, and if you are not ready to do that, then you are going to find that it is hard to keep control over your target.

And finally, there are some people who jump into the idea of manipulation in order to give them power, control, and everything that they imagined they ever wanted. And for some of these manipulators, that is exactly what they want and they couldn't be happier. On the other hand, there are some people who find that doing this manipulation is not going to give them what they want.

Think of it this way. Maybe you manipulated someone into a relationship with you and into saying they love you because you were looking for some attention and love from another person. You finally get into that relationship and get them to say those words. But it just isn't going to satisfy most people the way that they had hoped because they know that the other person was tricked into saying it. Yes, the target is going to say they did it on their own, but the manipulator knows the work they did behind the scenes to make those words come out. Sure, you technically got what you wanted out of the situation, but it just doesn't seem as satisfying when it is done this way.

As you can see here, there are a lot of different benefits that are going to come into play when it is time to use manipulation. And this is often why people will choose to work with manipulation in order to help them gain power, get control over someone else, and to get what they want out of life. But it is important to note that there are also going to be some negatives that come with manipulation, and it doesn't always work out the way that you would like. Understanding both sides of the story before you start to use these tools of manipulation can make a world of difference as well.

Chapter 4.   Mind Control Through NLP

At the point when you think of control, you consider somebody who thinks just about his very own needs, an individual who puts his responsibility for that of others. For example, babies, who are normally self-centered and persuaded of their supremacy, can be incredible controllers. They're canny enough to have made sense of Mom or Dad's hot catches, and they'll push those catches tenaciously to get precisely what they need.

Numerous grown-ups develop out of this kind of control. However, some don't. One of my friends concedes that she utilizes her emotions to twist others to her will. She essentially hasn't made sense of elective ways that would be progressively lovely for her and the remainder of us, to get what she needs.

Contrasted with manipulation, the influence is regarded to have an increasingly positive implication that mulls over others' needs and wants. As guardians, we need to impact our children to be sound and safe. As companions, we need to impact our companions to be happy and satisfied. As entrepreneurs, we need to impact our customers to be fruitful and prosperous. We need what is best for those in our range of prominence.

The concept of influence has numerous segments. It depends on solid affinity, clear and harmonious correspondence, and mindfulness and comprehension of others. We, as a whole, normally have these essential capacities somewhat. Be that as it may, similar to all aptitudes, we can figure out how to be better.

Back to the mallet. If you need to construct a house, don't you need the best hammer you can get? Would you ever think, "No doubt, I need to construct a house, yet I'm not going to utilize instruments". Would you stress that "if you use apparatuses to manufacture the house and figure out how to utilize them appropriately, would that be an unreasonable preferred position?" obviously not! If you need to be a successful influencer, NLP is perhaps the best instrument you can learn.

Would someone be able to figure out how to utilize a mallet to cause destruction? Absolutely. Might they be able to utilize NLP to control? That's right. In any case, through experience, that is extremely uncommon while gaining the NLP skills, there is an emphasize of the moral utilization of everything being equal. In all actuality, there is no "mind control" apparatus (except for extraordinary indoctrinating procedures) somebody could use to cause someone else to accomplish something unsuitable to their convictions or qualities.

In this book, we are emphasizing positive manipulation. That is why you have learned techniques such as building rapport. These help in building a connection and develop a solid relationship with people as well as on the corporate ladder. The manipulation that you do is meant to impact you with positive results, and also help the other person benefit. With this, they can come back for more of your services.

This book does not advocate for negative manipulation that will leave the other person drained and empty, while you gain what you want for your benefit. That will be destroying your relationships with people.

On the other hand, as much as we advocate for positive manipulation, we are aware that you do not have control of the people who aim at causing negative manipulation. In the following section, we shall look at some of the cautious activities that you can look out for to take note of a negative manipulator.

Spotting negative manipulation techniques

I have had a wide range of individuals attemp to "NLP" me into accommodation, including various individuals I've worked for over expanded timeframes, and even individuals I've been involved with. Thus, I've built up an entirely sharp insusceptible reaction to it. I've likewise examined its mechanics intently, generally to oppose the drivel of said individuals. Here's a couple of key strategies I've gotten.

Be very careful about individuals replicating your non-verbal communication.

In case you're conversing with someone who might be into NLP, and you see that they're sitting in the very same manner as you, or reflecting how you have your hands, test them by causing a couple of developments and checking whether they accomplish something very similar. Talented NLPers will be greater at covering this than more up to date ones. However, more current ones will, in every case, quickly duplicate a similar development. This is a decent time to call individuals on their poop.

Move your eyes in unpredictable movements at random times

This is cracking comical to do to troll NLPers. Particularly in the underlying phases of affinity acceptance, an NLP client will give extraordinarily close consideration to your eyes. You may believe this is because they're strongly keen on what you're stating. They are, yet not because they care about your musings: They're watching your eye developments to perceive how you store and access data. Shortly, they'll not exclusively have the option to tell when you're lying or causing something to up, they'll additionally have the option to make sense of what parts of your mind you're utilizing when you're talking, which would then be able to lead them to be so enlightened to what you're feeling that they nearly appear to be having some sort of mystic understanding into your deepest considerations. A cunning hack for this is simply to haphazardly dash your eyes around—admire the right, to one side, side to side, down, cause it to appear to be characteristic, however, do it arbitrarily and with no example. This will drive an NLP individual completely nuts since you'll be losing their adjustment.

Try not to give anyone a chance to contact you.

This is truly evident and sort of abandons saying when all is said in done. Be that as it may, suppose you're having a discussion with someone you know is into NLP, and you end up in an increased passionate state possibly you start snickering extremely hard, or get extremely furious, or something comparative and the individual you're conversing with contacts you while you're in that state. They may, for example, tap you on the shoulder. What simply occurred? They moored you with the goal that later if they need to return you to the state you were simply in, they can (or so the wayward rationale of NLP directs) contact you in a similar spot. Simply resemble, goodness hellfire no, you didn't.

Be careful about dubious language.

One of the essential methods that NLP noted is the utilization of obscure language to actuate sleep-inducing daze. Erickson found that the more ambiguous language is, the more it drives individuals into a stupor because there is less than an individual is subject to differ with or respond to. Then again, increasingly explicit language will remove an individual from a stupor.

Be careful about lenient language.

Words like "do not hesitate to unwind", "You're free to test drive this vehicle if you like it", "You can appreciate this as much as you can imagine, "Watch the f*k out for this." This was a significant understanding of pre-NLP trance specialists like Erickson: the most ideal approach to get someone to accomplish something, including going into a daze, is by enabling them to give you consent to do as such. Along these lines, gifted trance inducers will never order you inside and out to accomplish something, for example

"Go into a daze", they will make statements like "Don't hesitate to become as loose as you can imagine".

Be careful about nonsense.

Garbage phrases like "As you discharge this inclination increasingly more, you will end up moving into a present arrangement with the sound of your prosperity to an ever-increasing extent". This sort of hogwash is the bread and butter of the pacing-and-driving period of NLP; the trance inducer isn't saying anything, they're simply attempting to program your interior passionate states and move you towards where they need you to go. Continuously state "Would you be able to be increasingly explicit about that" or "Would you be able to clarify precisely what you mean?", this completes two things: it intrudes on this entire system, and it additionally powers the discussion into explicit language, breaking the stupor actuating utilization of obscure language we talked about in #4.

Figure out the real story.

NLP individuals will reliably utilize language with covered up or layered implications. For example: "Diet, sustenance and lay down with me are the most significant things, wouldn't you say?" superficially, if you heard this sentence rapidly, it would appear to be an undeniable proclamation that you would likely concur with absent a lot of thought. Indeed, diet, nourishment, and rest are significant things, sure, and this current individual's truly into being solid, which is incredible. Be that as it may, what's the layered-in message? "Diet, nourishment, and lay down with me are the most significant things, wouldn't you say?" Yep, and you just unwittingly consented to it. Talented NLPers can be unimaginably inconspicuous with this.

Watch your consideration.

Be cautious about daydreaming around NLP individuals— it's an encouragement to jump in with an oblivious prompt. Here's a model: An NLP client who was endeavoring to get me to compose for his blog for nothing saw I showed up not to focus and was investigating the separation, and afterward began utilizing the strategy recorded in #7 by discussing how he never needs to pay for anything since news sources send him audit duplicates of books and collections for nothing. "Everything for nothing", he started murmuring at me. "I get everything. For. Free." Obvious, no?

Try not to consent to anything.

If you wind up being directed to settle on a snappy choice on something and feel you're being guided, leave the circumstance. Hold up 24 hours before settling on any choices, particularly budgetary ones. Try not to give yourself a chance to get cleared up into settling on an enthusiastic choice in the spontaneous. Sales reps are equipped with NLP procedures explicitly for building hasty purchases. Try not to do it. Leave, and utilize your level headed personality.

Trust your instinct.

What's more, the principal and essential standard: If your gut reveals to you someone is screwing with you, or you feel uneasy around them, trust it. NLP individuals quite often appear "off", dodgy, or like trade-in vehicle sales reps. Escape, or solicitation, they show you the regard of not making a different NLP system while interfacing with you.

Mind control

Mind control methods are one thing and can be seductive and harmful depending on their use. For different people mean different things. These are also classified as coercive persuasion, brainwashing, change of thought, coercion, and seduction.

All the above terms have common features, particularly those that describe mental control. Nevertheless, each person refers to motivation and explicit or implicit control in a person's mind to take on a particular role. Then we will describe it in a reasonable amount of time and identify much of its strategies. Therefore, we'll ask you who needs to use them.

Could you change other people's minds? Can other people keep your mind under control? One common concern is that people can manipulate others ' minds without understanding them. This has contributed to the word mental control being typically found in theories, where anything from states to aliens is accused of controlling our ideas. The opinions of others can, of course, be affected, often strongly. Yet making them dance like marionettes for each wish seems highly unlikely.

Techniques of mind controls

Some techniques are normally used for mind controls. It does not just happen; there is a process that you, as an individual, should be aware of. Let us take a look.

In this section, we will examine some genuine mind control procedures that were customarily utilized by common individuals in personal connections as well as in gatherings.

The act of isolation

Physical disengagement can be extremely strong; however, in any event, when physical separation is not possible or not down to earth, controllers will regularly endeavor to confine you rationally. This might be accomplished in various manners from multi-week courses in the nation to condemning your family and friend network. Constraining some other impact by controlling the data stream is a definitive objective.

Having Criticism

Understand that criticism might be utilized as a disconnection tool. The controllers will ordinarily talk in terms of being them against others' terms, condemn the outside world, and guarantee their very own prevalence. As indicated by them, you should feel fortunate to be related to them.

Social evidence and pressure from peers.

The individuals who endeavor to control enormous gatherings of individuals will normally utilize social evidence and companion strain to mentally program newcomers. Social evidence is a mental wonder where (a few) individuals expect that the activities and convictions of others are suitable and, because "everybody does that", must be legitimized. This works particularly well when an individual isn't sure what to think, how to carry on, or what to do. Most individuals in such circumstances will take a gander at what others do and do likewise.

Is it possible to have positive manipulation?

No one wants to be negatively manipulated. Whether it's personal or academic life, the thought of being manipulated is usually something bad. Many of us equate it to negative associations, such as people who are trying to use us or drive people to do things they do not want to do. Have you ever even worried about the possibility of positive change manipulation? Today, we're going to look at how sometimes manipulation is a great thing as shocking as that may sounds. Manipulation has already been happening all around. Whether you know or not, in your professional and personal life, you are very likely to be exploited every day. Marketers and corporations around the world promote and unleash the power of coercion to get us to buy certain things and to live our lives in the same way.

Buy this shoe label.

Feed on more vegetables. Plant more crops.

Freedom from cigarettes.

Support this political party. Vote that way.

What are the good and bad cases of manipulation? Would it be wrong to persuade people to abandon cigarettes or to follow a healthier lifestyle, or can we interpret it as something positive?

Good leaders are often searching for ways to involve and inspire their staff. It is an essential part of staff career development, with a lot of benefits both for individuals and companies.

Positive management of your employees can be an effective management tool. Using a constructive form of manipulation to inspire workers to achieve their objectives will help improve their performance and encourage teams to achieve the goals of the organization.

A scholar sums up the gaps between persuasion and manipulation, saying it lies in all of these three things:

- The intention underlying the effort to convince that person.
- Authenticity and honesty.
- The net benefits or effect on that individual.

Always have a conversation with yourself, reflecting on your intention of wanting to manipulate people and how truthful and transparent is your process. You should know whether or not the actions were for that individual's good.

As a boss or employer, it's important to preserve your beliefs and always have an ethical impact on your workers. This form of good manipulation is often used by non-profit organizations and ethics firms to try to persuade individuals to act, support others in need, and promote positive changes in the world. There is a discussion in an essay about controlling people for good that individuals can alter human behavior. But you may be wondering what is the way this energy can be used? How do you use psychology to ethically convince people? Non-profit and non-governmental organizations use persuasion to draw donations and raise money and increase awareness of critical issues that require action and reform.

Dread of estrangement

The new members of the manipulative gatherings will, for the most part, get a warm greet and will shape various new companionships that appear to be a lot further and more important than anything they have ever experienced. Later on, if any questions emerge, these connections will turn into an integral asset to hold them in the gathering. Regardless of whether they aren't persuaded, the life in the outside world may appear to be somehow lonely.

Reiteration

Consistent redundancy is another ground-breaking influence instrument. Even though it might appear to be too oversimplified to possibly be powerful, yet rehashing the same message, again and again, makes it natural and simpler to be remembered. At the point when reiteration is joined with social confirmation, it conveys the message without failure.

The presence of personal growth techniques is another confirmation of the power of repetition. If you can convince yourself through reiteration, odds are somebody may endeavor to utilize redundancy to control you into speculation and carrying on with a specific goal in mind.

Tiredness

Being tired and lack of sleep can bring about physical and mental tiredness. At the point where you are physically worn out and less alarm, you are increasingly defenseless to influence. A study referenced in the Journal of Experimental Psychology shows that people who had not rested for just 21 hours were increasingly helpless to the recommendation.

Framing new personality

At last, controllers need to re-characterize your personality. They need you to quit acting naturally and become a robot, somebody who thoughtlessly pursues their requests. Utilizing all strategies and mind-control systems referenced above, they will endeavor to remove an admission from you — some type of affirmation that you accept that they are great individuals accomplishing something to be thankful for (slight varieties are conceivable). At the outset, it may be something immaterial like concurring that the individuals from the gathering are fun and cherishing individuals or that a portion of their perspectives are, in reality, substantial. When you acknowledge that one seemingly insignificant detail, you might be progressively prepared to acknowledge another and afterward another and another. Before you know it, out of wanting to be steady with what you do and say, you start recognizing as one of the gatherings. This is especially amazing on the off chance that you realize that your admissions were recorded, just before you overlook it, there is a physical verification of your new character.

How do you succeed in manipulating people's minds

The use of hypnotism is a powerful tool. In less than a minute, a professional hypnotist could bring somebody in motion to get someone to take care of his suggestions.

In counseling, entertainment, marketing, and even seduction, hypnosis can be used. If someone is hypnotized for treatment or entertainment, it is easy to be conscious of it and even allow the hypnotizer to trance.

It takes a completely different, persistent bag of tricks to hypnotize people in a conversational context, to get them to obey your advice without realizing that you use your "unique abilities" on them.

It is what it is called hypnosis of covertness and communication. This is the tactic used by master salesmen, leaders, and seduction specialists to get people to do everything they desired. Such hypnotic methods are so effective that they could even seem to manipulate the brain.

You may be concerned about how this hypnosis can secretly work.

The very first step you should do is to link to the person you want to hypnotize; this connection is called "analysis" by some. This state of compatibility with the subject must be preserved. This can be done orally and with the correct body language. When done correctly, the subject experiences a profound psychological bond with the hypnotist.

Once you find a source with and have a relationship with the subject, the next move is to strengthen this sense of confidence and comprehension, thus increasing any mental protections and becoming more receptive to suggestions.

Once you have a strong connection with the subject, it's time to inject secret recommendations into his unconscious, which is also called embodied instructions. There you "ask" whatever you want him to do, but you could just "tell" him as you do during a typical session of hypnosis.

Critical thinking will be triggered by being responsive and clear to suggestions. Critical thinking will increase the defenses and barriers of the natural mind, and block direct orders you send him.

So how do you propose the topic once you have them in your spell?

You do this with metaphors and orders embodied. So what does that mean exactly? Hypnotic symbols or sequences are hypnotic documents specifically designed. To circumvent critical thinking obstacles, they use hypnotic scripts and send suggestions or orders directly to the subconscious. This tricks the audience into thinking that we take something trivial when we are speaking about something else, which is the real meaning of the metaphor.

Chapter 5.   The Power of NLP

NLP or in full neurological programming is a way people communicate with others through psychological means. This basically means that this mode of communication looks at the brain and how it functions generally. This statement is transpired from the name of the communication mode which is the neurological part. Every human has his or her own way of how the brain works and reacts to different circumstances. This communication mode then is different in everyone depending on gender, race, age and even in groups formed by people. This whole model of communication calls to show that opinions and matters are different in everyone. They also may be the same but vary in intensity. Everyone's brain is programmed or set differently and thus every human should be respected due to that small and significant fact.

The NLP model of communication has the way it works. It may be successful based on how the person who wants to use it takes it at hand. This mode of communication is mainly used by professionals and those are the psychiatrists. Since their work is to understand human emotions and how the body and mind work together, this mode of communication is suitable for their use. They try to understand the human day to day lives affect the mind and its work.

So, one might ask, how does the brain work together with or in conjunction with the body? First of all, the brain functions to the call or responses made by the human body. This also applies to animal bodies and brains from different animal classes and kingdoms. When a body part is in need of something it sends a defined message to the brain in which the brain response appropriately. This explains how the body and mind are set to work together even though they are very different from each other.

Brain activities can be understood and read by people through going through the brain waves. These waves explain high and low activity in the brain of a particular person. These waves help someone see clearly how human beings work. What do I mean? I mean that the body has different parts which must work together to bring harmony and great being in human beings. Psychiatrist read and understand the brain waves. They also give someone their problems and how to fix them in the long run of everything.

To understand fully the communication mode connected with the brain one has to understand the brain and communication separately. Communication thus is the art of talking and understanding what others are saying. The nature of communication is the sender to the receiver then receiver to sender. Communication quite frankly is easy to understand and use. Communication happens every day and everywhere. This is happening in animals, plants, and people too. Communication hence is universal among all the people, animal, and plants. There are also different ways to communicate but that is beside the point at hand today and here. Communication is a great root for living a healthy and prosperous life.

Communication is affected by the brain each and every time. So how does the brain affect communication at large? This is very simple. The brain before any signs or symbols is depicted in a communication triangle, the brain filters and works on the next cause of action for each and every situation. This shows how communication is complex and very well organized in human beings and animals.

Communication is also special and very interesting depending on the topic being discussed and how the topic itself is being handled by the people discussing it at large.

Finally, how do we understand and use NLP in our normal daily lives? This is a good question to keep one to understand the usefulness of communication and the brain. In this kind of communication, the brain is key. It is in the center of all communication so all the responses are made and clarified in the brain or at a part of its lobe. NLP makes communication in all understanding easier to remember without wondering how it happens and in what manner in all respect to the communication. This type of communication is only suitable for all the people trained and specialized in the understanding of the human brain or even the animal brain or even both might work. The NLP is not for everyone's use but for the chosen few. This makes it limited to a very few numbers of individuals and subjects since it is mainly done to the subjects who give their consent to it.

Chapter 6.   What Is Hypnosis

Hypnosis is susceptibility of the mind to suggestions. Despite this state, a person under hypnosis subconsciously knows what is being done except that he/she allows these things to happen.

A common application of hypnosis is hypnotherapy, which aims at improving a well-being. You cannot inflict damage to a person in a hypnotized state. Even in such a state, a person can react to danger. The mind has defense mechanisms that are hard to understand.

The practice of hypnosis has been around for so many centuries. Lately, scientists have devoted time to study and explain how and why it is possible. Many theories arise regarding the different practices of hypnosis. Here are the truths about hypnosis.

Hypnosis is a natural, inherent trait.

It happens to everyone, in some form or another. You may not recognize it or may even deny that you witness at least once or maybe more. Every person may drift in and out of the hypnosis state.

For example, you are reading a novel. You are so engrossed with the story that you do not "hear" your significant other asking you a question. Your conscious mind may not register the question but you know you are being asked. In some way, it resembles hypnosis.

Since it is a natural trait, a hypnotized person is not at risk of getting stuck in one state or another. They naturally drift to a waking state or deep sleep. Thus, hypnosis is not dangerous. The experience is like listening to a boring speech and zoning out until the speaker finishes. Some may feel disoriented but such feelings do not last.

Hypnosis is not a sleep state.

Although the word hypnosis comes from the Greek word "Hypnos" which means sleep, it does not constitute the normal sleep state. Hypnosis state seems like you are asleep but your mind is aware, awake and responsive. You hear everything. Your senses heighten.

Hypnosis does not make a person weak-willed.

A hypnotized person is susceptible to suggestions, but it does not mean they are weak-willed. They remain in control. In fact, they can stop hypnosis anytime they want.

If hypnosis makes a person weak-willed, hypnotists could abuse such power over a hypnotized person. A lot of hypnotists could command a person to do everything they say. Fortunately, a hypnotized person remains in control despite his/her high susceptibility to suggestions.

Relaxation is not a prerequisite to hypnosis.

You can hypnotize a person anywhere, anytime, provided that person is willing. You may even do it during a strenuous activity. Hypnosis can bring relaxation but relaxation is not a prerequisite.

Hypnosis does not cause permanent amnesia.

A hypnotist can command a person to forget, for the time being, what has transpired. This allows the mind to process the events subconsciously. In the long run, a previously hypnotized person can remember the hypnosis in great detail.

Hypnosis is different from a trance state.

Many hypnotists have difficulty identifying the difference between hypnotic and trance state. Most of the times, these two words are used interchangeably. The only similarities between the two are the heightened senses and highly efficient mind.

Hypnosis deals with heightened susceptibility of the mind, most likely the subconscious part. Trance state targets both the conscious and subconscious.

Hypnosis can happen to anyone. As mentioned, hypnosis is innate to all. Everyone experiences it very often. Only a small percentage of the population is not hypnotizable. Being hypnotizable is not dependent on personality traits.

Concepts of Hypnosis

Before learning the different techniques of hypnosis, you must understand the different concepts, how the mind works and how people communicate and behave. This is imperative to make hypnosis effective and efficient.

The human mind is a complex mechanism. Learning these concepts enables you to hypnotize anyone, anytime. Understanding these hypnosis concepts helps you recognize which technique to use.

Power of Suggestion

Sometimes, people act based on someone else's suggestions. This power of suggestion is what advertisers use to convince consumers to buy a product. Hypnotists also use this power of suggestion to induce hypnosis.

The most common example of the power of suggestion is the placebo effect. This is a suggestion during the waking state. Doctors, nurses, pharmacists apply this power of suggestion to patients. The doctors would sometimes give an ordinary pill to patients. Believing that this pill cures their diseases, the patients feel better. Why? The doctors suggested that the particular pill can heal them.

Combined with the power of language, the power of suggestion creates expectations. It creates a powerful way of making the hypnotized person's move towards his or her dominant thoughts.

Power of Imagination

The human mind is capable of unlimited imagination. Together with the power of suggestion, you can create endless possibilities with your hypnosis.

Visualization scripts include the power of imagination. This power helps people achieve something or anything close to their physical limitations or beyond their normal capabilities.

Conscious vs. the Subconscious

In psychology, the mind can function on conscious and subconscious levels. The conscious part is what you can control. The conscious mind makes decisions, thinks logically, and performs cognitive functions. It is the origin of willpower and the recorder of short-term memory. It dwells in the past, present and the future.

On the other hand, the subconscious mind controls body functions and automatic reactions and reflexes. It does not think in executing an action. Like a computer program, once hitting the run button, the subconscious automatically executes whatever actions a particular body part or organ has to do. Examples are breathing and blinking.

The subconscious mind is the seat of habit and long-term memory. It does not change so easily. Embedded memories, actions, and reactions in the subconscious take time (or years) for newer ones to replace them. The subconscious controls self-preservation mechanisms. This is the reason hypnotists cannot make a person to do something bad while hypnotized.

The mind generalizes and filters events, actions, objects or anything seen, felt, heard, tasted, and experienced. Generalization is the ability of the mind to think in blocks or concepts. It makes thinking quicker especially in times of danger. Filtering is the ability to block sensory inputs and delete negative mental images.

Language Patterns

Hypnotists use language patterns to hypnotize other people. These patterns include dissociation, supposition, double binds, metaphors, embedded commands, exploration, and anticipation.

Use of Metaphors

Metaphorical language pattern is an excellent way to make other people trust you. They can relate to what you are saying without the feeling of intrusion in their personal lives. With metaphors, you can speak about the lives of your targets and still be confident that you can hypnotize them.

Double Binds

This language pattern offers choices, usually two, to your subjects or targets. Whatever the answer is, the outcome is the same. Most of the time double binds language pattern is only answerable with a yes or no.

Embedded Commands

In this language pattern, you are commanding other people do what you want them to do. It is usually used in an authoritarian method of inducing hypnosis. However, scrutinizing closely induction scripts, all induction techniques, except non-verbal method, use embedded commands to deliver suggestions and ask permissions.

Dissociation

This pattern uses an out of the body experience. Many people fall into a dissociation state when they experience stress and traumatic events. This dissociation seems to be a natural response of most people. Dissociation happens naturally during hypnosis. You can utilize this natural occurrence to hypnotize other people.

The Laws of the Mind

Thoughts affect the body. If the mind thinks you are strong, the body seems to follow. This is the reason constant emotional stress weakens the body. You can use this law to induce hypnosis. If your targets think that hypnosis is possible, they are more susceptible than those people who are skeptical.

Concentrated attention

The more you think of something, the more it becomes a reality. For an instance, constant, repeated imagination of wanting to become more sociable or efficient in work will make your conscious mind believe it. As a result, you find ways to achieve it.

However, for people who have difficulty separating between reality and imagination, concentrated attention has a negative effect. These people sometimes live in a world that is a protected cocoon.

In hypnosis, you can use this law of the mind to hypnotize anyone and strengthen your suggestions to your subjects. Concentrated attention makes your targets believe in anything you suggest them to do.

Dominant effect

People create habit over time. They hold on to this habit to rationalize behavior and thoughts. Once an idea is embedded in the mind, it takes time for this to be replaced by a new one. For new ideas to replace old ones, people need strong emotional connection or consequences.

Association

The opposite of dissociation, people sometimes feel when they can relate such emotions with something. For example, classical music relaxes the mind while metal rock music evokes harsh and negative vibes.

Reverse Effect

This law proposes that the conscious mind cannot force the subconscious to follow. The greater is the effort of the conscious mind to understand or remember something the harder it is for the subconscious to response.

Negation

The mind does not know how to compute negation. When you say do not think of this or that, the first thing the mind does is to think of this or that. For example, do not imagine that this elephant is colored in violet. The mind interprets it as "see the elephant, it is violet."

Compounding

This law utilizes the compounding effect of repeated suggestions. Every time you make the same suggestions over and over again to the same person with only slight variations, you are creating a pattern. On the succeeding hypnosis, induction is easier than the first to third sessions.

Core Beliefs

Core beliefs are created early in life. These beliefs determine who you are and what you are in life. However, every core belief does not define all aspects of your life. One core belief may define how you deal with your social life but not how you manage your work environment.

These core beliefs are consistent with the rest of your life but can be altered through hypnosis, will power and by other life changing events. These beliefs play a big role in retaining long term problems in your life.

Understanding these personal core beliefs will help you in knowing exactly how to hypnotize anyone.

Phases of Hypnosis

Hypnosis involves preparation, planning, and implementation. Even in covert or stage hypnosis, you need these to execute a flawless act. Each act of hypnosis involves stages.

Phase One: Pre-talk/Pre-Hypnosis

This phase involves talking to other people about the things you are going to do to hypnotize them. Tell them what to expect and that hypnosis is safe. Elaborate to your targets that even if the session is interrupted, nothing will happen to them. They will just fall into deep natural sleep or wake up like nothing happened. They may feel a bit disoriented but the disorientation will fade in a few minutes or so. During this phase, expect high resistance from people you are planning to hypnotize.

Pre-talk is necessary for hypnosis. Even stage hypnotists talk to their audience for a few minutes before they actually hypnotize the person. Stage or covert hypnotists ask permission before they actually induce hypnosis. In most cases of a street or covert hypnosis, long pre-talk is not necessary. All you need to ask is if the target believes in hypnosis and if he/she is willing to try. In other instances, you won't need a pre-talk.

While you are talking to your target, make observations. A successful hypnosis depends on how keen you are to other people's behavior. Know when they avert their eyes while you ask them about hypnosis.

Phase Two: Hypnosis

This phase involves the formal application of the induction technique that works on people. If the technique does not work, the person may have a higher resistance than you have expected. Revise your hypnosis program accordingly based on your new observations. Alternatively, you will need to practice more. When hypnosis is successful, include deepening tests to ascertain the depth of the hypnosis state of your subjects.

Phase Three: Post Hypnosis

Professional hypnotists and hypnotherapists use post-hypnotic suggestions and talks to fortify their suggestions and programming session. In your case, you can use post-hypnotic suggestion to tell to your target to forget what you did.

Usually, hypnotists use post hypnosis to help other people make changes in their lives. Use this opportunity to help other people, to dispel any mistrust that people have in hypnosis. If you have asked your target on the pre-talk about hypnotizing him/her, reassure the person that the hypnosis went well and that you achieve the expected results. If you did not ask whether your targets believe in hypnosis or not, thank him/her for his/her valuable time.

Use the principle of post-hypnotic talk to evaluate your hypnosis sessions with people. Write your observations and the techniques that work and that do not work`. Evaluate the personalities of the people who are susceptible to hypnosis and those who are not.

You can use this information to improve your talents.

How do you know if you can easily hypnotize anyone?

Hypnotizing a person you know through daily interactions is easier since you already have an idea about how he/she behaves with stress or with suggestions. You already have an initial assessment of how resistant he/she could be with hypnosis.

From time to time, perhaps you have tried asking these people their views on hypnosis. Some might have told that hypnosis is just a work of too much watching movies. Others might have answered that they do not believe in it or that they are not hypnotizable.

With strangers you have never met, thinking of the proper technique is daunting. You might not even contemplate of trying hypnosis with people you do not know but trying hypnosis with strangers can be most fulfilling.

Before hypnotizing strangers in the street, practice with the people you know well and people you are merely acquainted with. As you gradually go out of your comfort zone, you realize that hypnotizing anyone is as easy as learning your ABCs and numbers.

Remember, the more you practice, the more likely you succeed in hypnotizing even the most resilient person.

Myths About Hypnosis

Dispelling the many stereotypes of hypnosis is the first step in understanding this area of psychotherapy. The sideshow practitioner with a big moustache who dangles or spins a large object with a spiral design in front of the patient until they fall under his spell occurs only in movies.

- Myth #1—Patients cannot remember what happens during hypnosis.

It is not true that patients under hypnosis cannot remember anything when they are pulled back out of the hypnotic state. Patients under hypnosis are generally fully aware of everything during hypnosis and remember everything that occurs during a session.

In some cases, as when a hypnotherapist suggests to the patient that he or she forgets certain things that occurred immediately before or during a session, the patient may experience posthypnotic amnesia, but this effect may result from a deliberate effort to help the patient recover from a psychological difficulty, and in most cases it is limited and temporary. Amnesia has been reported in some cases, but it is very rare.

- Myth #2—Hypnosis can help patients remember forgotten events.

Television crime shows often portray the power of psychics and hypnotherapists to solve crimes by helping

89

traumatized victims recall details from the crime scene that allow lawyers and police officers to crack the case, but the idea that hypnosis can help patients retrieve forgotten details or memories of past events has been largely disproven.

There is some evidence that hypnosis can help improve memory overall. However, studies have shown that in instances in which hypnosis has been used to help patients retrieve lost memories or achieve so-called "past life regression", the results were more likely false memories or fictitious recollections resulting from suggestions during the trance state.

- Myth #3—Hypnotherapists can put you under a spell and make you do anything.

It is a myth that anyone can be hypnotized against their will or forced to act in ways that violate their beliefs or morality. In order for hypnosis to be effective, the patient must be a willing and active participant. Similarly, when the patient is fully hypnotized, the hypnotist does not have complete control over the actions of the patient under hypnosis. People who are hypnotized may be less inhibited to act in certain ways, but even in a trance state, patients are not able to act in ways they believe are wrong or that violate their morals or ethics.

- Myth #4—Hypnosis can give patients superhuman abilities.

Popular culture sometimes portrays the limitless possibilities that can open up to patients who undergo hypnosis. Film and television may portray hypnotherapy sessions in which the patient is convinced that when he or she comes out of the trance state, they will be able to run faster than a car, be smarter than anyone else at work, lift automobiles, or resist bullets. Hypnotherapy can help patients improve their performance in a variety of areas— both physical and mental. But it cannot allow anyone to exceed the limits of their own physical or intellectual abilities.

Facts About Hypnosis

In actual practice, hypnotherapy is much less dramatic and exciting than the portrayals in popular film and television. In fact, many people enter a hypnotic state every day. A hypnotic state is defined as a very relaxed and focused psychological state in which the subject is very calm, focused, susceptible to suggestion, and less likely to be influenced by hesitations or inhibitions.

For example, every time you sit down at home or in a movie theater to watch a film, you enter a hypnotic state. As the movie begins, your mind shifts its attention from concerns about work, family, relationships, bills, and other daily concerns to the story that is about to unfold. Especially if the lights are dimmed and outside interference from sounds and activity is muffled or blocked, your mind gradually relaxes and begins to shift its focus more and more to the film, until at some point you are entirely engrossed by the images, sounds, and events on the screen. Often during these episodes, we enter such a deep state of hypnosis that we react to scenes of violence, comedy, or shock as if they were actually happening.

In professional environments, many contemporary work gurus have developed the idea of "flow." When you are at work and so focused on what you are doing that it ceases to require any strain or effort, you have entered a state of "flow." When you are in this state, you are capable of producing high quality work that may normally seem excessively difficult. What's more, you may be able to sustain this high level of productivity for hours on end and even derive an intense sense of pleasure and happiness. This, too, is a state of hypnosis.

Hypnosis is usually used in combination with psychotherapy. During psychotherapy, patients may have explored many of the painful or difficult thoughts or feelings they have been experiencing. Under hypnosis, they may be more willing to explore these areas in more depth, which can lead to a better resolution. There are two main types of hypnosis:

• Suggestion therapy: This type of hypnosis uses suggestions to help patients change their behavior, as with smoking or overeating, or to change their perceptions, as in cases when patients are experiencing pain and discomfort.

• Analysis therapy: This type of hypnosis is used to put patients in a deep state of relaxation, so they will feel more willing to discuss some of the thoughts and feelings that may be hidden in their subconscious mind. This type of hypnosis can be used to help treat psychological and mood disorders, especially when it is used just prior to a session of psychotherapy.

What is Conversational Hypnosis?

Conversational hypnosis is the attempt to communicate with a person's conscious mind and keep them from knowing that they are being hypnotized. It is a term commonly used in the medical world to refer to the process of studying a person's mind. The aim is usually to alter or change the way a person behaves or believes in their subconscious mind so that the target person acknowledges they changed their mind on their own without any medical or psychological procedures.

Why Do You Need to Learn Conversational Hypnosis?

Conversational hypnosis is a significant factor in today's life. It is used in most aspects of life, for instance, when you are in market places, you might find yourself buying something you never intended to because of a compelling seller. You, later on, ask yourself how it happened because it feels likes it was all a dream. That is the power of conversational hypnosis.

So why do you need to learn conversational hypnosis? From the example above, we can see that it can be used to convince and persuade people. When your career or job involves trying to convince people, like a lawyer or a salesman, then you need to learn conversational hypnosis. This is an excellent way of winning over people and manipulating them your way.

 A study done by Gross International supports this ideology; it revealed that it is easier to convince an individual through conversational hypnosis than any other method. Another reason you should learn it, is that it puts you in a better position to understand what other people prefer and are thinking about. Getting into someone's mindset and figuring out how they feel is an excellent method to figure out their reasoning.

For instance, if you are a salesperson, you will need to figure out how a potential client prefers before approaching them with your product. You cannot contact an older adult with a set of youthful, trendy pairs of shoes; they will most likely reject it.

The Ethics of Using Conversational Hypnosis

Discussed below are the ethics of conversational hypnosis:

Fear: There are a host of fears associated with hypnosis that as much as there is a basis for them, they are often practiced in cases of misinformed agitations that iron out the danger at hand. Another ethic associated with conversational hypnosis is that the hypnotist has total control over the person they are hypnotizing, including what they do or what they think. They can see they manipulate what the person is thinking and the way they are behaving.

Post-hypnotic effects: The post-hypotonic results are many times deliberated for therapeutic purposes. This ethic of conversational hypnosis says the hypnotized person might do something dangerous to themselves or others around them after the hypnosis session that wasn't intended by the hypnotist — for instance, mentioning a trigger word that makes them fall asleep when doing something that requires high concentration like driving a car.

What is NLP & Ericksonian Hypnosis?

NLP refers to the act of knowing how people have organized their thinking, emotions, behavior, and language to produce the results and scores they do. It gives people a method to modify the best performances achieved by leaders and geniuses in their respective fields. NLP is also widely applied in personal development as well as to accelerate success in business establishments.

Ericksonian Hypnosis is an indirect hypnosis method named after the great Dr. Milton Erickson, a famous American psychiatrist. He is massively regarded as the founder of hypnotherapy. He discovered a host of ways that are now widely used in various fields, from therapy to neuro-linguistic programming. He found that indirect suggestion results in therapeutic behavioral change. He suggested conversations with clients should be made using contradictions, metaphors, and symbols to influence how they behave instead of giving them direct orders.

Steps of Conversational Hypnosis

The first step in conversational hypnosis is the foundation of your education. It pertains to all the concepts and analogies that hold together your hypnosis. The second step is creating the right environment or rather the hypnotic atmosphere. You will merely be adding to ideologies and concepts in step one. The third step involves introducing the element of solidarity in your process. This is done by advancing on the skills you already learned in the previous stages.

In step four, you will introduce the piggyback induction. You will use multiple topics and sets to help move the focus from an external view to an internal one. Step five involves adding yet another induction, the trance voice induction. It consists of establishing trance voices, including the unconscious and conscious minds.

In step six, you will refine the process even further by applying sensory reach descriptions and stories to your suggestions and the trance themes. This is done through using the sensory descriptions and other learned story skills acquired from your studies. Moving on to step seven, you will start to implement and incorporate the frame controls. It will involve all the framing features of sustaining your frame and deframing them as well.

Step eight involves adding more inductions in your processes again. You can use the trance models and formulae, you know, including the COMILLA and PCAT formulas. You will then be able to add more memories and hypnotic suggestions, beginning with the most sophisticated processes at that point. Lastly, step nine, which is the final one, will see you add a nested loop in the first eight steps. You can use all the necessary and master level loops.

Chapter 7.   Practical Use of Hypnosis

Patients under hypnosis feel calm and relaxed and are generally more open to suggestions. The main uses of hypnosis are for resolving problems associated with physical illnesses, behavioral problems, and psychological ailments.

Physical conditions

Hypnotherapy can help patients who are having difficulty with any of the following physical illnesses:

Chronic or acute pain

Many patients who have been diagnosed with rheumatoid arthritis or post-surgical pain have benefited from hypnotherapy by altering the patients' perception of pain. In one experiment, a patient under hypnosis was instructed not to feel any pain in his arm. The patient then placed his arm in a tub of very cold ice water and was able to leave it therefore several minutes without experiencing any pain. Patients in the same experiment who had not been hypnotized had to remove their arms from the water after only a few seconds.

Pain associated with medical procedures

Patients who are undergoing dental care, childbirth, or other painful medical procedures have benefited from undergoing hypnotherapy prior to treatment.

Migraine headaches

Because migraine headaches are often triggered by stressful conditions, hypnotherapy can help reduce their frequency and intensity without the side effects of medication.

Irritable bowel syndrome (IBS)

This condition can cause considerable discomfort. Although not effective as a long-term treatment on its own, hypnotherapy can help patients resolve short-term discomfort associated with IBS.

Side effects from cancer treatment

Chemotherapy to treat certain forms of cancer can cause considerable discomfort and nausea. Hypnotherapy has been effective in helping some patients alleviate these side effects.

Skin conditions, including warts, psoriasis, and eczema

Some skin conditions can be triggered by stress and anxiety. In these cases, helping patients find a way to resolve chronic anxiety can help relieve symptoms.

Behavioral changes

Hypnosis can also be used to effect behavioral changes, such as in treatments for the following conditions:

Insomnia

Patients suffering from insomnia may also be suffering from stress-related conditions. Hypnotherapy can help patients learn new habits and techniques to help the patient fall asleep without medication.

Smoking, overeating, bed-wetting

Addictions and other behavioral problems can be difficult to resolve using only therapy and medication. Hypnosis can help patients learn to change their behavior in areas where they have been resistant.

Emotional and psychological disorders

Finally, hypnotherapy is sometimes used to treat the mental health problems listed below.

Stress and anxiety

Stress and anxiety disorders are often treated with medication. However, such treatment may only address symptoms and may result in harmful side effects. Hypnosis can provide an additional source **of relief for patients suffering from this condition.**

Phobias

Phobias are a difficult and complex area of psychology. Though there is no single answer for why someone may have developed a certain fear, hypnotherapy can help the patient change his or her perceptions and reactions to triggers.

Post-traumatic Stress Disorder

Also known as PTSD, this condition is similar to stress and anxiety disorders but usually caused by an acute or sudden traumatic experience. The effects can cause long-term problems and hypnotherapy can help patients find healthier ways of responding.

Grief and loss

Grief and loss can lead to ongoing challenges for many people. By helping patients refocus their attention, hypnotherapy can aid in a quicker recovery.

Depression

There are many causes of depression. Sometimes patients have been in difficult circumstances, while others may be psychologically predisposed to depression, Often, it is a combination of factors. Regardless, hypnosis can help patients redirect their mental focus and find relief.

Dementia

Patients with dementia may have trouble concentrating and remembering. Hypnosis has been shown to be effective at helping them reconnect with familiar surroundings.

Attention Deficit and Hyperactivity Disorder (ADHD)

The growing concerns about this psychological ailment have resulted from the quickened and disjointed pace of work and life in environments that use digital technology and video. Hypnosis can help patients adjust to a less stressful setting and develop a longer attention span.

What Happens During Hypnotherapy?

During a typical session of hypnotherapy, the therapist will begin reviewing the patient's goals for treatment. Once you and the therapist are clear about the reasons for seeking hypnotherapy, he or she will begin talking in a calm, soothing, and gentle voice, usually describing images and scenes to help the patient relax and feel safe. This initial step is designed to create what is called a "receptive state" in the mind of the patient. Once the therapist sees you have attained this state of relaxation and receptivity, he or she will begin suggesting ways you might achieve your goals. These suggestions may include constructing visual images in your mind in which you see yourself successfully attaining the behavior or condition you have identified as your goal.

For example, the session may begin with the therapist asking you to close your eyes, relax, and let go of any tension. Depending on the personal information you have shared with your therapist, they may then begin to suggest locations or events that you associate with feelings of safety, relaxation, and calm—maybe the beach or the ocean, a room in your home, or some type of music or activity.

Once the patient has achieved a trance state, which is described as a state between sleep and wakefulness, the hypnotherapist can make suggestions. If the therapist suggests that you are eating a cheeseburger, you may experience the meal and taste of a cheeseburger, if the therapist suggests that your nose is heavily congested from a cold, you may alter your voice when you talk. Alternatively, the therapist may ask deep and probing questions about a sensitive area of your life that you normally are uncomfortable discussing. In a hypnotic state, you may find it much easier to open up.

Throughout the session of hypnotherapy, the patient feels a complete lifting of inhibitions. He or she will be very suggestible and willing to act in ways that normally be embarrassing or uncomfortable. Yet, at no time does the patient lose consciousness or forget that he or she is engaged in a session with the hypnotherapist. The effectiveness of hypnotherapy lies in its ability to induce the patient to enter a state in which their inhibitions have been lowered so that the psychological defenses they have built up no longer prevent them from saying or doing things that can help them resolve their problem. With enough practice and training, many patients are eventually able to practice self-hypnosis as part of a program of ongoing self-care.

Is Hypnotherapy Effective?

As discussed above, hypnosis is used in a fairly limited number of situations to help people cope with pain, stress, depression, grief, or anxiety; certain physical ailments like irritable bowel syndrome; overcome the effects of chemotherapy associated with cancer treatment; or to effect behavioral changes such as quitting smoking and losing weight.

Generally, although hypnotherapy has been recognized as having valid and proven clinical results, it is still viewed as a supplementary or secondary line of treatment following a full program of psychotherapy or cognitive behavioral therapy.

In addition, some people are more likely to benefit from hypnotherapy than others. People who exhibit higher levels of activity in the prefrontal cortex, the anterior cingulate cortex, and the parietal regions of the brain are more likely to be suggestible under hypnosis. These areas of the brain regulate functions such as memory, perception, emotions, and task learning. Overall, researchers have developed the following statistical analysis of the effectiveness of hypnosis in the general population:

- Approximately 15% of people report high degrees of responsiveness to hypnosis.

- Approximately 10% of adults are resistant to hypnosis or impossible to hypnotize.

- People who exhibit the capacity to indulge in fantasies generally experience more benefit from hypnosis.

- Children are usually easier to hypnotize than adults.

Drawbacks of Hypnotherapy

In certain cases, hypnosis may actually cause harm.

For example, patients with symptoms of psychopathy or who experience hallucinations or delusions may be hard to control or may experience a worsening of their condition under hypnosis. Some psychiatric disorders may require the use of medication, and in these cases, hypnosis may be an ineffective treatment. Hypnosis is also not recommended for patients who are currently abusing substances or under the influence of drugs or alcohol.

Patients who wish to use hypnosis as a method of pain control should be examined by a physician first to ensure they are not experiencing any serious problems that may require surgical or medical intervention.

Finally, due to hypnotherapy's ability to cause the patient to create false or fictitious memories or to experience strong emotions, using hypnosis to treat patients with serious psychological disorders, such as those outlined in the Dark Triad or other dissociative disorders, is generally regarded as potentially harmful and dangerous.

Chapter 8.   Personal Benefits of Mind Control and Manipulation

The idea behind being a persuasive person, the main objective of persuasion, is to get something in return. There is no sense in practicing the art of persuasion if there is nothing desired in return. Persuasion means to cause someone to do something specific. Therefore, some sort of gain is desired, some sort of end result.

In order to know the intended end result of the persuasive effort, there must be a defined desired outcome. The person doing the persuading wants something tangible, something definable. But what do they want? Well, that is completely up to them to decide. But they must decide, before engaging in any form of persuasion, exactly what they hope to achieve at the end of the conversation.

This is what is meant as defining desired outcomes. The thing that is desired must be decided before any kind of persuasive tactics begin so that the person doing the persuading understands the desired outcome.

Pretend the office is holding a meeting to decide the location of a new office. The old office is small and cramped. The business is growing and needs more room to be able to continue to grow. So an office meeting will take place where, hopefully, the new location will be decided upon. This is the first step in defining the desired outcome, knowing what the proposed outcome is. In this case, it is the location of the new office.

So the meeting has been set for a particular time and place. Finished, right? Wrong. Without some sort of order and organization, the meeting will be unproductive and the desired outcome probably will not happen. The meeting is crucial to the desired outcome. Without some sort of specific plan then the meeting is nothing more than people in an office meeting in one room to make conversation.

So now it is necessary to set up the meeting; to have a plan as to how the meeting will proceed. Since this is a meeting of the entire office, there is no need to decide who to invite since everyone will be in attendance. So the next step is to create the agenda for the meeting. Will there be time for questions? Will certain people be invited to participate by offering specific recommendations for the new location? How will the ultimate decision be reached? All these factors need to be decided before the meeting begins.

When beginning the meeting be sure to mention the desired outcome. Let everyone know exactly what they are there to discuss. Make sure everyone involved knows and understand the desired outcome. Set a specific time for discussion and a time when the decision will be made. Then when the meeting is reaching the end of its prescribed time restate the objective and determine if a decision can be made or if more research is needed.

An outcome is nothing more than an end result that can be seen and measures. It is the consequence of the action. It is the conclusion that comes from persuading someone to do something. In any desired outcome there are four things that will need to be decided before the desired outcome can be decided upon. Those four things are: is something specific desired, is something already owned needing to be kept, who should be connected with and how, and what skills are needed to achieve the desired outcome.

It is important to decide these things because the underlying objectives will definitely affect the way the outcome is to be gained. It is similar to a football game where there is a defensive team and an offensive team. One group attacks the opposing team and one group defends against the attacks from the opposing teams. Each team will have a different set of priorities and procedures. Their desired outcomes will be quite different from one another. Each team will need to decide what it is they want to learn, defend, or acquire. The goal will determine the game plan.

Some sort of change needed has been identified and will be achieved. The path to achievement begins with setting a goal. The end of this journey is the desired outcome. It is necessary to understand that these are two separate entities that work together to achieve a result.

A goal is a destination. An outcome is a specific thing; it can be seen and measured. While setting the goal is vital to receiving the outcome, they are two quite different things and should be treated as such.

Goals always have reasons behind them. Something that is thought of as being necessary to happiness, to wealth, to health, or just because it is truly desired, is just not there. Whatever the reason is, it is that exact reason that drives forward progress toward the desired outcome. In order to be able to progress, to go forward to the goal, that goal and the idea of achieving it must be firmly entrenched in your mind. Without a steady focus on the goal, there is no possibility that the goal will ever be reached.

Imagine going to work every day for fifteen years, doing the same job every day. Imagine this is a job that needed college courses, so it was a chosen job. During the past fifteen years, doing the same job every day has been rewarding and profitable. There have been several promotions, the last of which came with a private secretary and a lovely large office. Several other people, who have not been working here quite as long, are now the team that directly reports every Monday in this large new office.

But going to work has become somewhat boring. The job just does not bring the amount of satisfaction it once did. The problem is not in the job itself but in the person doing the job. What seemed so right all those years ago now feels so wrong. What is really desired is more interaction with people. In managing other people, a new skill has emerged:

the ability to take raw recruits and mold them into productive team members with a bright future. That is the job that brings happiness and satisfaction.

But while this thought has been firmly entrenched in the mind for months now, no changes have been made to get closer to the goal of that type of occupation. And so every Monday morning is filled with team meetings, every day is filled with spreadsheets, and every Friday is filled with boundless joy that another work week has passed. Why?

The answer to Why? Is procrastination. Whether intentional or unintentional, procrastination has ruined many good intentions. Unintentional procrastination does happen sometimes. Everyone has that moment of "oops, I forgot to take care of that today I'll get to it first thing in the morning." That is unintentional; something was forgotten. Intentional procrastination means knowing something needs to be done but putting it off until whenever. Many people do this with dreams and desires, especially those that will require extra work to accomplish or simply just a big leap of faith. Changing careers when one is firmly established is a scary thing. But what someone wants at twenty may not necessarily be what they want at forty.

People change. Their hearts change. They must be willing to follow their dreams and make them a reality. But people procrastinate out of fear.

So ask these three questions:

- What exactly am I afraid of? Do I fear to lose a great job that will pay for my kid's college and not being able to find one that pays as well? What if I have to take a pay cut and can no longer pay the mortgage? What happens if I lose my health insurance? These are all valid questions that must be addressed when considering a large change in employment.

- What will I gain if I am able to conquer this fear? What great gain will be realized? Will it be a new job, a new career that is more in line with current life goals? Maybe the real dream is the chance to help other people.

- What do I do to fight this fear? Accept the fear as real. Acknowledge its existence. Then make a plan to reach the new goal and proceed without waiting. Go forward without procrastination.

Now, it is time to set a goal to make this dream a reality. Identify the goal as specifically as possible. The more specific the goal, the better the chance is to realize that goal. Vague goals are nothing more than wishes. It is as simple as the difference between "I want to lose weight" and "I want to lose twenty pounds." The second statement is a specific goal that can be measured as work toward it progresses.

Know exactly what is desired as a reward when the goal is achieved. If the goal is weight loss, perhaps the reward is being able to wear that dress featured in the store window. If the goal is learning how to swim, then maybe the goal is to swim in the ocean for the first time ever. Plan how this goal will be achieved. Think about the senses that will be used along the way and how they will make this progress easier or more difficult.

Visualize the plan and try to imagine any possible obstacles. That does not mean putting the obstacles in the path, but in being aware of the possibility that they might crop up and having a plan to deal with them. If the intended goal involves weight loss, what will be the plan for coping with the buffet during the holiday season? If the goal is to complete classes online then what happens if the internet goes out or the computer crashes? It is necessary to have a back-up plan to deal with life's little emergencies.

What will be used for markers along the way to track progress toward the goal? If the goal is weight loss, then perhaps a wall chart with every five pounds lost marked in red. Perhaps a drawing of a thermometer, with the goal being the mercury bulb at the top, and the thermometer is filled in gradually with every pound lost. Have a system in place to track these milestones.

Be aware that working toward any goal might come with negatives attached. Changing careers will most certainly mean a change in income. What if the career change means moving to another state? Is that a viable option? An extreme amount of weight loss will mean constantly refreshing the wardrobe. It is important to be aware of anything that might be seen as a negative effect of reaching the goal. These must be acceptable or the goal will need to be changed.

And when little distractions occur along the way, do not let them cancel out any progress that has already been made.

Life happens. All roads have bumps in them. Even Shakespeare knew that no matter how good the plan was, it might not work. So acknowledge the fact that little bumps in the road will happen and have a plan to overcome them. Maybe it was a temporary lapse in judgement. Maybe it is a sign that the current path needs to take a bit of a different direction. The choice is solely up to the person who set the goal and created the path. And when the goal is reached, so will be the desired outcome.

Chapter 9.   Difference Between Manipulation and Persuasion

Manipulation is a way to control others, and it can be used in different ways. Some of these ways can be very subtle, and others can be easily recognizable, especially if you know what you are looking for.

With manipulation, one of the first things that a person will notice is the feeling of fear, obligation and/or guilt. When someone is trying to manipulate you, they are trying to coerce you to do something that you don't want to do. You feel scared thinking about doing what they want or feeling scared in the act, there is a feeling of obligation that goes along with it, and you sometimes feel guilty if you don't do it at all.

The two types of manipulators that can make you feel this way are known as a bully and a victim. When someone bullies you, they are often using fear in the form of aggression, threats, and intimidation to make you do what they want.

On the other hand, if they play the victim, they try to make you think that they are hurt. No matter the case, they are often the ones who caused the problem in the first place. If you are being targeted by a manipulator who is playing the victim, you will do whatever they want to stop their suffering. You might even feel responsible for their suffering, even though you are not.

Another thing a person who is being manipulated does is question themselves and what they are doing. This can often be referred to as gaslighting. This type of manipulation has people not only questioning themselves but what is real to them, what they perceive, their own thoughts, and even their memory. Has someone ever twisted your words around and made it about them? Have they taken over the conversation to make you feel like you're the perpetrator and that you did something wrong while you wonder what it is that you exactly did? Gaslighters know how to make their victims feel a false sense of guilt, responsibility and even defensiveness. They will have you questioning if you have done something wrong when you haven't at all.

Another manipulation tactic comes with strings attached. People should want to do things for you just because they want to and not what they can get out of it. This is one of the most common forms of manipulation. You feel like someone is being nice to you and doing things for you when you need them. But there always seems to be a catch or something involved. If you don't adhere to those stipulations, then they make you feel ungrateful, like you are taking advantage of their kindness.

There are other forms of manipulation, but these are the most common forms. It is imperative to know what manipulation is and the different forms so that you can protect yourself against it.

Manipulation is not the only control tactic that we should watch out for. Persuasion is another form of control used against people daily. Persuasion can be found in images, sounds and even through the use of words. There is a deliberate attempt to influence others. One of the key points about persuasion is that people are not coerced or manipulated; instead, they are free to choose what they believe. Even though the images, sounds or words used in advertisements help them choose what others tell them too. Persuasion can be found in advertisements or messages on radio, the internet, television, billboards, and face to face communication through verbal and non-verbal ways.

This technique has increased over the years and especially in the 21st century. Messages in the form of advertisements over different sorts of media have grown and are spread rather rapidly. On average, every U.S. adult is exposed to 300 to 3,000 advertisements every day (Cherry, 2018).

It can even be found within business itself, and we are not talking about advertising agencies. There are a lot of companies that use the art of persuasion to sell goods and services.

Many of the advertisements that we see have been specially made or crafted to get people to buy their products or services because they want to look like them or live that certain lifestyle.

If both manipulation and persuasion are prevalent in advertising, then what are their core differences?

How can you tell them apart?

"Advertising manipulates when it encourages the audience to form untrue beliefs" (Noggle, 2018). This occurs when we are told that fried chicken is healthy, or when the associations that are used are often faulty, like Marlboro cigarettes and the association with the ruggedness of the Marlboro Man. If the manipulation of the Marlboro man is successful, the ads themselves contribute to disease and death. People often think of manipulation as wrong because it harms the person being manipulated. And, this is the case most of the time. But there are times when manipulation itself is not harmful.

What makes manipulation wrong?

In any situation, the manipulator tries to get the other person to believe what the manipulator feels is wrong. The manipulator is lying to the other person, and to make the other person make some form of mistake. Thus, they can also make you believe a false statement, make you feel inappropriate, get someone else's approval in the wrong way or to doubt something, even yourself. There is no good reason to get someone to doubt. So, to answer the question above, the core distinction between manipulation and non-manipulation depends on the manipulator and if they are trying to get someone to make some sort of mistake regarding how they feel, think, doubt, or pay attention to something.

Reasonable persuasion, defined by Immanuel Kant, is the only moral way to influence people. Persuasion is something we all experience, as well as do, every single day. If it is reasonable, then it is not evil. It is just considered to be one of the ways that we interact with everyone around us. You might want to persuade someone to think a certain way because you want to see the world become a better place. This is often true when you are debating with someone about their political view of the world and you come back with an intelligent, researched argument that changes their perception. Did you harm them in any way? No, you reasonably persuaded them to come to your side. They made the choice all on their own.

Another way that you can persuade someone is through making a profit. All types of persuasion further some sort of self-interest. There is nothing wrong with making money. It isn't evil, unethical or immoral. However, you have to persuade another person to part with their money by getting them to believe that what you have to sell – whether it is a good or service – is what they want or need.

Jonathan Fields states that the difference between persuasion and manipulation can be defined in three ways:

- The intent behind the reason you want to persuade someone
- The truth behind the process
- The benefit of impact on the person you are trying to persuade

For example, Amber married Devon 2 years ago, and they started to have marital problems during the beginning of their second year of marriage. One-night Devon came home drunk and hit Amber in the face. The abuse continues from there until one night she wakes up in the hospital with broken bones. Amber's parents are sitting beside the bed, and her mother takes her hand in hers. That night her parents urge her to leave Devon because it is in her best interest. They know she loves him, but he needs to get help for his anger. They persuade her to file domestic violence charges against him because the next time she might not be so lucky, and they can't lose their baby girl.

Now Amber has a choice in all of this. She has the choice to stay with Devon and risk that things will get better or worse. Or she has the choice to leave him with or without pressing charges. Her parent's argument was reasonably persuasive, but they were still giving her a choice. They did not force her or influence her to make a choice. There were quite a few ways, as was stated before, to manipulate the situation and make her do what they wanted, even if that wasn't what she wanted, which would be manipulation. There is no good type of manipulation, only good persuasion.

Amber isn't dumb and knows what she is risking if she goes back to Devon. And, this is where the persuasion influences her to make a choice. The argument her parents brought to her is with love and compassion. They care about her well-being, and they want her to know that she can come home, and everything will be okay. Amber feels good making this decision and is not making it out of remorse, guilt or out of obligation to her family. This is the main and very important difference between persuasion and manipulation.

This is why it is important to know the difference. When you are persuading someone, they often are feeling better for meeting you. Those who are being manipulated, feel guilt the second you leave.

Chapter 10.   Psychological Persuasion Techniques

The distinction between persuasion and dark persuasion is the intention behind each activity. A persuasive person may be convincing another person to do something without having to think of the tactics to use or having a motivation. Dark persuaders, on the other hand, understand their intentions and have a bigger picture behind what they are doing. They know their victims and what motivates them to apply some tactics in persuading them.

Common Dark Persuasion Tactics

There are several common techniques that dark persuaders use to persuade their victims successfully. The persuaders are well aware of their victims and will tactfully apply the methods to get what they want.

Foot in the Door

This is more of a principle that many dark persuaders follow. They ask their victims for smaller favors before asking for bigger favors. They first ask for something little that will make you committed to helping them. The persuader then continues to ask for something bigger, which will be a way of continuing with something you had technically agreed on. Dark persuaders are aware that asking for small favors will increase their chances of agreement to more prominent support.

Anchoring

Dark persuaders use the technique to influence the decisions you are about to make. You can be a victim of dark persuasion in instances when you are purchasing a product. To determine its value, you can compare its price to a similar product and decide from there. Anchoring is a very powerful technique used by salespeople to persuade their customers to buy a product. For instance, when looking to buy a new motorbike and come across a good deal for 13000$. You bargain with the salesperson, and they agree to lower the cost to 10000$. You will go home feeling satisfied, and contempt in thinking of how well you bargained. However, it is possible the value of the motorbike was even lower than 10000$, and the initial price of 13000$ acted as an anchor to persuade you to purchase it. You end up getting convinced that anything lower than the initial price is a good deal.

Commitment and Consistency

Dark persuaders believe that people will always remain consistent in their beliefs and actions. They are sure that making a victim be committed to a small request increases the chances of using the first commitment to influencing them to do more. They do this by first asking you whether you support a certain deal. When you agree, they will make another request that will make you feel obliged to act on it because you showed your commitment.

Authority

Habitual dark persuaders focus on authority in any subject or field. They make their victims feel they are a source of authority. They act superior to coerce other people to do as they want for their benefits. For instance, a person who has a twitter handle and would like to gain more followers, they may convince people of how rich they are and make them follow them to learn the tactics of getting rich.

Scarcity and Demand

This is one of the most commonly used technique by dark persuaders. Salespeople and marketers are habitual users of this technique to persuade people to buy their products. They use the scarcity technique as a target for people who prefer purchasing goods that are in low supply. They will convince a customer that the particular product is available for some limited time or that its supply is very low.

Reciprocation

Human beings will always feel the obligation of returning favors. Dark persuaders are aware that people will always give something in return regardless of whether it will be pleasing. Dark persuasion involves making a victim indebted to them. They consistently make statements or act in a way that increases the chances of the victim, giving them something they need in return. An example is when a salesperson dealing with oranges gives a piece of orange for a customer to taste. The customer will feel indebted and end up purchasing oranges even though they did not intend to.

Dark Seduction

Dark seduction involves the use of coercive and manipulative techniques to get other people like you. There are various techniques used in dark seduction. These include:

- **Choosing the Right Victim**

The art of dark seduction is dependent on the seduction target. Dark seducers tend to thoroughly study their prey and select those that seem much susceptible to their seduction charms.

- **Creating a False Sense of Security**

Approaching Indirectly- Dark seducers tactfully approach their targets because when they do it directly, their motives will not be fulfilled. They consider approaching a target at an angle that makes them eventually know who they are. They focus on coming up with a neutral relationship gradually moving from a mutual friend to becoming a lover. They instill some feelings of security to the target and finally strike with their motives.

- **Appearing to be an Object of Desire**

Creating Triangles- Dark seducers follow the analogy that people will always be attracted to those who have attracted the interest of others. To draw their victims closer, dark seducers make people hunger for their possession. People will be enticed to act in the best possible way to become the center of attention. They do this to try and win the dark seducer from the group of admirers.

Tips to Help You Avoid Being a Subject of Dark Seduction

Be Alert

Always consider looking at your surroundings to establish the kind of people around you. Dark seducers are likely to identify their targets easily.

Walk with Purpose

Dark seducers are likely to identify people who seem confused and make them their targets. Walk like you are aware of where you are going.

Do Not Allow People to Stop You

Dark seducers will do anything possible to make people fall into their traps. Do not be too easy to stop a stranger anytime they ask you to. Just keep moving and do not follow strangers.

Closely Watch Your Body Language

Ensure you walk in an organized way. This is because dark seducers will target people who show fear and physical vulnerability as they walk.

Conclusion

Manipulation is being used in every area of life; from TV to advertisements. While some forms might not be as cynical as others, manipulation in relationships and inter-personal relationships causes more problems than one might think. Equipped with the right tools, you can now spot manipulation and put an end to it before it harms you.

Since manipulation is so prevalent in our world, it's hard to avoid it altogether. But, keeping an eye and ear out can help you find those in your life that are more interested in their own needs and using you to get them.

Remember, don't allow yourself to stoop to their level. The best payback is to show them that you can live your own life without their influence. Burst their bubble when you see right through their manipulation tactics. That hurts them the most when they can't manipulate you to get what they want.